Chat-up Lines

Stewart Ferris

summersdale

Summersdale Publishers Ltd

46 West Street

Chichester

PO19 1RP   UK

www.summersdale.com

ISBN 1 84024 179 9

Printed and bound in Great Britain.

I can read you like a book. I bet you're great between the covers.

I'm not letting you anywhere near my spine.

What winks and is great in bed?

I don't know.

(Wink)

What would you say is the best thing about being so gorgeous?

Not being expected to talk to ugly people like you.

People tell me I've got a one track mind, but the track is heading straight for you, babe. Shall we pull into the sidings and couple?

No thanks. I don't want to spoil a pleasant day by talking to you.

It must be my birthday because the sight of you is the most important gift I've ever had.

What about your natural gift for repulsing women?

I'd like to father your children.

Fine, they're over there.

Would you like me to lick
champagne out of your navel?

There isn't any in it.

You've turned my floppy disk
into a hard drive.

*Sorry, I don't date men
with tiny peripherals.*

What time would
you like me to set
the alarm for in the morning?

I don't care.
My boyfriend always gets me up.

I'd like to make love to you.

I'd rather we skipped straight to the
post-coital fag.

Would you like me to
get into your knickers?

*There's already one arsehole in there,
and that's plenty.*

Where have you been all my life?

*What do you mean – I wasn't
even born for the first half of it.*

Would you like a f**k . . .

No.

. . . ing drink?

Do you want to come back to
my place for a pizza and a shag?

No thanks, I don't like pizza.

Do you sleep on your stomach?

No.

Can I, then?

Bond. James Bond.

Off. Piss off.

It's getting late. Why don't
we have a shag?

No thanks, I'm too tired.

Well why don't you lie down
while I have one?

The doctor said I should release
my fluids regularly. Would you mind if I
used your body as a receptacle?

I'll lend you a cup.

Your face or mine?

His.

Hey, don't go yet . . .
you've forgotten something.

What?

Me.

What sign were you born under?

'No entry'.

Excuse me, I'm new around here.
Can you give me directions to your
bedroom?

*I'm not very good with directions.
You'd better ask my boyfriend.*

Wow.

Yuk.

Would you like to come back to my place for a bacardi and grope?

Just a gin and platonic, please.

Can you tell me the time, because I want to make a note of the moment we first met?

I'll give it to you twice, because it's also the moment we split up.

Excuse me, aren't we related?

No, and I don't want to be.

I know a great way to burn off
the calories in that sandwich you've
just eaten.

*Yes, me too, and it involves
running away from you.*

You have the bluest eyes I've ever seen.

*Thanks. I only had them
resprayed yesterday.*

You look like you've never
done it in a water bed.

You look like you've never done it.

When I was a prisoner of war they
tortured me on the rack, and it wasn't
just my legs they stretched . . .

What else, then – your imagination?

Can I phone you for a date?
What's your number?

It's in the phone book.

But you haven't told me your name.

That's in the phone book, too.

Underneath these clothes
I'm completely naked.

Prove it . . . to someone else.

You're utterly beautiful, but there must be something about you that's less than perfect: I expect you're a hopeless cook.

True, so I suppose Nature's compensated you with perfect cooking abilities, then?

You remind me of the last person
I went out with.

That must be going back a bit.

Have you ever
experienced puppy love?

No, only pigeon-holing and
monkey-spanking.

The best thing about you
would have to be my arms.

*Thanks – I would offer to shag your
brains out, but it looks as if
someone has beaten me to it.*

Excuse me, is your body real?

No. You have to inflate it through my mouth every ten minutes.

Can I count on your vote?

I doubt if you can even count.

(Call her over using your finger)
I made you come using just one finger. Imagine what I could do with my whole hand!

Can you make yourself come with just one finger?

I think the sun shines out of your arse.

Well, you're living proof that even a turd can be polished.

Do you know the difference between
fellatio and focusing?

No.

Would you mind helping me adjust my
telephoto lens, then?

Are you free tomorrow night?

*No, but I'm on special
offer the day after.*

Congratulations! You've won first prize
in a competition: a date with me!

Oh. What was second prize?
Two dates with you?

Will you call me pretty soon?

I doubt it – you're not pretty now and
I'd be surprised if that ever changed.

I'd go through anything for you.

Great, the exit's just over there.

If I could see you naked, I'd die happy.

If I could see you naked, I'd die.

Can I spend the evening with you?

I gave up baby-sitting years ago.

Can I buy you a drink?

I'd rather just have the cash.

What's a girl like you doing
in a place like this?

Trying to avoid you.

Save me – I'm drowning
in a sea of love!

Tough, I can't swim.

You and me would look sweet
together on a wedding cake.

Only once you'd been cut in half.

You look good enough to eat.

What a shame you need to diet, then.

When I look at you,
I know I've caught the love bug.

It's a pity you weren't inoculated.

Take that jacket off and
let me look at your spine.

*Come any closer and I'll
throw the book at you.*

I'd like to run my fingers
through your hair.

You can wipe the lice on my sleeve.

Seeing you makes my heart beat
uncontrollably fast.

The sight of you gives me heart burn.

If you were a building you would be Versailles Palace.

And you'd be a shed.

Do you believe in magic?

I used to, until I realised I can't make you disappear.

Do you believe in
love at first sight?

No.

We could make
beautiful music together.

*I'll just fetch my
earplugs, actually.*

I have designs on you.

*I think you'd better go back
to the drawing board.*

Can I bury my head
in your cleavage?

Just bury your head.

You're the one I've been
waiting for all my life.

Let's hope you die young.

You bring me out in a hot sweat.

You bring me out in an allergic rash.

I could get lost in your eyes.

*That's conjunctivitis,
it makes them a little foggy.*

Will you come out with me?

*Out of the closet, certainly, because
meeting you has helped
me confirm my sexuality.*

I want to be really
dirty with you.

*You smell as if
you already are.*

Am I the light
of your life?

No, you're far too dim.

You make my
heart skip a beat.

*Only one? I was banking on
a cardiac arrest.*

I want to f**k you
over and over again.

I want to f**k you over.

When should I phone you?

Whenever I'm not there.

I'm like quick-drying cement: after I've been laid it doesn't take me long to get hard.

I'd rather go to bed with a packet of cement.

With me you need never
fake an orgasm again.

*With you I'd rather just fake
the whole thing.*

I don't expect to have sex with you on
our first date. I'm quite restrained.

*Well I'm even more restrained.
I don't even expect to have
a first date with you.*

Sorry if I'm dribbling, but I had
to get drunk before I could
come and talk to you.

*It's funny how pigs don't
turn into men when they drink.*

If you go out with me I'll treat you even
better than my sports car.

*What, a good servicing every ten
thousand miles or every ten months,
whichever comes first?*

Where do you come from?

Way above your league.

Why don't we have a holiday romance?

*Most men like you remind me
of holidays . . . they never seem
to be long enough.*

Are you as hot as me?

*I'm fine actually, but perhaps you
should get some air to your brain
by undoing your flies?*

Shall we go to your place or mine?

*Both. You go to yours
and I'll go to mine.*

Let's be honest with each other . . .
we've both come here
for the same reasons.

Yes, you're right.
Let's go and pull some girls.

You're most beautiful looking
person I've ever seen.

So what makes you think
I would want to talk to you, then?

When I'm with you
I feel like a real man.

So do I.

Would you go crazy if I
went out with you for a couple of
months and then left you?

*I'd go crazy if you went out with me for
a couple of months and* didn't *leave.*

If we went on a date, how would you describe me to your friends?

If I was desperate enough to date you, I wouldn't have any friends.

You'd probably regret it in the morning if we slept together, I suppose. So how about we sleep together in the afternoon?

Your approach wasn't bad, but I'd rather see your departure.

Excuse me, were you looking
at me just then?

*Yes, I thought from a distance you were
good looking. Sorry, I forgot my glasses.*

Can I be your love slave?

Well I certainly wouldn't pay you.

You've got such a heavenly body that
I've named a star after you.

*By the look of your body I wouldn't be
surprised if someone had named a
bouncy castle after you.*

Look, I won't beat about your bush, I
just want to get something fairly big
between us.

How about the Atlantic Ocean?

I've always been fascinated by beautiful women. Mind if I study you?

Let's make it a joint project: I've always been fascinated by ugly men.

Hi, look, I'm not going to be able to date you tomorrow night, so why don't we squeeze one in tonight instead?

By the looks of you I doubt that it would be much of a squeeze.

I can fulfil your sexual fantasy.

Where's your horse, then?

Excuse me, would you help me
with an itch that I can't reach?

*Sure, just rub it against the
lock on my chastity belt.*

Can you help me? I had sex with
someone last night, and I think it
might have been you.

No, I think it was with yourself.

You know, being a millionaire
can be pretty lonely without someone
to share it with.

*I'll share your money with you,
if you like.*

Hello, you don't know me, but I've just come back from the future in which you and me have the most passionate love affair. And it started tonight, actually.

And I've just come back from even further in the future where I found out that we're brother and sister, so let's change history, shall we?

I'm sure I've noticed you before.

I'm not sure I've even noticed you yet.

Hi, I'm from Wonderbra. We're conducting free spot checks to make sure our customers are wearing the correct size bras. Just breathe out slowly once my hands are in place . . .

When you've done I'd better check your underpants. You look as if you could benefit from a smaller pair.

I feel like I already know you because I've undressed you completely in my mind. Nice body – I'd like to see more.

I did the same, but I wasn't impressed.

Would you like to go to
bed with me tonight?

I can't – I haven't anything to wear.

I've got a condom
with your name on it.

You must be mistaken.
My name's not Durex Extra Small.

Would you ever wear real animal fur?

*I would if it provided an extra layer
between me and you.*

Would you like to come to a
concert with me?

I've got the CD.

I'm trying to break the world kissing record for snogging the most beautiful women in one evening. Can I kiss you?

Yes, but only because I'm trying to snog as many ugly men as possible tonight, and you would be worth double points.

You've got great boobs.

So have you.

You really set me on fire.

*Oh good, I didn't think I
used enough petrol.*

If love is a drug, I'm addicted to you.

I recommend cold turkey.

What's your birthstone?

Breezeblock.

My body's like a temple.

*I'd have said it was more like an
amusement park.*

I could really turn you on.

It's no big deal. I can do it myself just by not thinking about you.

Would you like to come for a meal with me next week?

I've eaten.

Mind if I take your picture?

Where to?

Can I take you on a shopping trip?

*Wouldn't you rather just
take me in bed?*

Can I wash your car for you?

I don't think your hose would reach.

Would you like to come to a nudist
camp with me – I could show you
what I've got to offer?

*I could see that sort of thing
in a packet of shrimps.*

Would you like to come to bed with me?
I've got an electric blanket.

*Why don't you come home with me
instead? I've got an electric chair.*

Would you like to watch a
sunset with me?

I've already seen one.

Can I fill you up, madam?

Unleaded, please.

Can I tickle your tonsils?

I think the surgeon has chucked them out.

Let me have a quick stroke.

Sure, shall I call the ambulance?

I'd like to have your children.

Go ahead and take them.

People think I'm a policeman because of the size of my love truncheon.

Yes, I remember 'Inch High Private Eye'.

My yacht is stranded here for a few days until the weather improves. Want to keep me company on it?

That depends on the size of your tender.

Will you hold my beer while
I go to the toilet?

Not while it's coming out, thank you.

I don't think I've seen you
for about ten years.

*Well make the most of it, because
with a bit of luck I won't see you
for another ten.*

Will you help me
choose some garden
furniture at the weekend?

I've already chosen some.

I'd like to jump into a bed with you.

OK, what about that flower bed?

Do you want to go
clubbing with me?

*Great, where can
we find some seals?*

You take my breath away.

*I try, but you keep
on breathing again.*

Can I look up your skirt?

*Certainly. Here's the catalogue.
It's on page 57.*

Would you like to come
for a drink with me next week?

I'm not thirsty.

Can I pinch your bum?

Can I pinch your wallet?

You're irresistible.

You're resistible.

Didn't we meet in a past life?

*Yes, and I wouldn't
shag you then, either.*

Would you like to come to a hilltop
with me next week to watch the
return of a comet that hasn't been
visible for the last thousand years?

I've seen it.

Are you a policeman, or am I wrong in thinking that's a truncheon?

Both . . . I am a policeman, and it's not a truncheon.

How would you like my eggs in the morning?

Fertilised, please.

What's it like being the most
attractive person here?

You'll never know.

The more I drink, the prettier you get.

*There isn't enough alcohol on the planet
to make me find you attractive.*

I think we should leave together for the sake of the other women . . . you're making them look ugly.

Good idea. You're making the men look too good.

There's something on your face, I think it's beauty. Let me try and get it off . . . oh, it's not coming off.

Beauty shares the same characteristics as my bra. It's not coming off.

You make me melt like ice cream, you make me boil like a kettle, and you make me gurgle like the morning after a curry.

You need medical attention.

Let me put some fizz into your life.

OK, start by fixing my Sodastream.

I may be a bit of an eyesore, but beauty is only a light switch away.

You owe me a drink: you're so ugly I dropped my glass when I saw you.

Wasn't that you on the cover of Cosmo?

Yes, but I've finished sitting on it now. Want to borrow it?

I like to think it's my vocation to make women happy in bed.

Let me guess: you deliver meals on wheels to the bed-bound?

I'd like to demonstrate to you the sexual equivalent of a marathon.

Go ahead. I'll just watch from over there.

You make me drunk with passion,
intoxicated with love, and
inebriated with desire.

*Are you absolutely sure it's got
nothing to do with the ten pints
you've drunk tonight?*

Can I see your tits?

No, they've just migrated.

Do you want to play my organ?

Only if it's got some good rhythms.

Has anyone ever told you
how beautiful you are?

Yes, loads of people.

I've had part of my body pierced.
Would you like to know which bit?

Your brain.

Why not be original and say yes?

No.

I could make you the
happiest woman on earth.

*Why, are you about
to go into space?*

I'd like to marry you.

*I'd rather skip straight
towards the divorce.*

I'm a postman, so you can rely
on me to deliver a large package.

*Sorry, but I need someone who comes
more than once a day.*

I bet you a drink that
you won't kiss me.

You win. Here's a drink.

You're cute.

My cute what?

I bet you my watch that you
won't let me grope you.

You win. Here's my watch.

Do you believe in love at first sight, or
should I walk past you again?

Get yourself some sturdy walking boots.

I bet you my car that you
won't have sex with me.

You win. Here's my car key.

Shall I open the door for you?

I'd rather you waited until we land.

I bet you my chest that you
won't take your bra off.

Sorry, I'm not playing anymore.

Would you like my seat?

I didn't realise transplant surgery was so advanced.

Hey, it's you! I nearly didn't recognise you with your clothes on. Oh, sorry, I thought you were an ex-lover.

And I thought you were a future lover . . . until you opened your mouth.

Hello, I'm your cake. Would you
like to have it or eat it?

*I'm not hungry. I think I'll just
give it to the dog.*

I'm thinking of giving celibacy a try.

Not with me, you're not.

What radio station would you
like me to switch on in the morning?

Hospital radio.

Mind if I plug my lap-top
into your modem socket?

*Isn't amazing how small they
can make them, these days?*

I'm a helicopter pilot: fancy
riding my chopper?

I'd rather just shag you.

If you kiss me I promise not
to turn into a frog.

*Why would I want
to kiss you, then?*

When I was a prisoner of war,
held captive in a tower, the other
men used part of me to climb down
the wall and escape.

Oh no, not you again?

I think it's time we
introduced ourselves.

I already know myself.

I was planning on having sex tonight.
Would you like to join me?

*I can't make it tonight. You'll have to
make it a rehearsal.*

If I kissed you I'd go weak at the knees.

*That's probably because I'd have just
given you a good kicking.*

You're very attractive even though
if you were any more vacuous
your head would implode.

*If you were a little bit more intelligent
you'd still be stupid.*

If I told you I was well endowed
in the undercarriage department,
would you shag me?

No.

THE LITTLE BOOK OF CHAT-UP LINES

If you were food, you'd be caviar. If you were a word you'd be serendipity. If you were a car you'd be a Rolls Royce.

*If you were a real man
I might stay and talk to you.*

Are you cold, or are you smuggling tic-tacs inside your bra?

Are you cold or are you smuggling a tic-tac inside your underpants?

You remind me of a squirrel. I'd like to pile my nuts up against you.

You remind me of a rat, and I've already called the Pest Control department.

Would you like to see something swell?

Yes, the bruise I'm about to inflict on your face.

I love you.

I love chocolate, but I wouldn't bother chatting it up.

What would you say to a little f**k?

*Leave me alone, little f**k.*

Nice legs. When do they open?

Nice mouth. When does it shut?

Would you like to join me?

Why, are you falling apart?

Would you like to come
and meet my family?

OK, when are the opening hours?

Is that a gun in your pocket
or are you just pleased to see me?

No, it's a gun.

Hi there. I'd like to ask you what's your
idea of a perfect evening?

*The one I was having
before you came over.*

I'm a meteorologist, and I'd like to study
your warm front. Let's go to an isobar
and have a drink.

*No thanks — I've seen the forecast.
Damp in parts, hot and sticky with rising
cumulo nimbus. I think I'll stay at home.*

Are your legs tired? You've been
running through my mind all day.

Yeh — I was looking for a brain cell.

If you should happen to fall in love with
me, I'll be waiting for you.

*If I ever get that desperate
I won't be worth waiting for.*

Try imagining you're in love with me.

My imagination doesn't stretch that far.

Do you think it was fate
that brought us together?

No. It was just bad luck.

Would you like to come out
with me for some coq au vin?

What sort of van do you drive?

When I look at the stars I see your eyes.
When I look at a flower I smell your
perfume. When I look at the sun I feel
your warmth.

When I look at a cow I see your bullshit.

What would you say is my best feature?

Your ornamental pond.

I'm considering chucking my girlfriend for you. How do you feel about that?

But I don't want your girlfriend.

Can I have your name?

Why — haven't you already got one?

I've always believed in love at first sight.

So did I — until I met you.

Can I kiss you?

*Of course, but mind you don't burn
yourself on my cigarette.*

Do you mind if I smoke?

I don't care if you burn.

Hello. Didn't we sleep together once?
Or was it twice?

*It must have been once. I never make
the same mistake twice.*

You would be great to go on a camping
holiday with. Separate tents, of course.

I'd prefer separate campsites.

I've got some condoms, so I think we should sleep together right now.

What's the hurry? Are they close to their expiry date?

Do you kiss with your eyes closed?

I would if I were kissing you.

Shall we go all the way?

*Yes, as long as it's
in different directions.*

Would you accept if I
were to ask you out?

Accept what — defeat?

You don't sweat much for a fat lass.

*I will when I start
running away from you.*

I'd like to see more of you.

There isn't any more of me.

I think I could make you very happy.

Why, are you leaving?

Go on, don't be shy: ask me out.

OK, get out.

Didn't we used to be lovers?

Yes. I left you because you have an infuriating memory problem.

I don't remember that.

Will you come out with me on Saturday?

Sorry, I'm having a headache at the weekend.

You look like my fourth wife.

How many have you had?

Three.

I'd go to the ends
of the world for you.

*Yes, but would
you stay there?*

Let's skip the awkward beginning and
pretend that we have known each other
for a while. So, how's your Mum?

*She told me I wasn't
to see you any more.*

Is your daddy a thief?

No.

Then how did he steal the stars out of
the sky and put them in your eyes?

Is your daddy a thief?

Yes.

Can he get me a cheap DVD player?

Before I buy you a drink,
can you tell me if you like me?

*Get the drink first. We'll deal
with the bad news later.*

How did you get to be so beautiful?

I must have been given your share.

May I have the pleasure of this dance?

No, I'd like some pleasure too.

I've been given a couple of
tickets for the play on Thursday
— do you want to come?

Only if you give me both of them.

I'm a doctor: what's your appendix
doing tonight? I'd love to take it out.

*Very funny. You should be on the
television then I could turn you off.*

Going so soon? Stay a minute
and let me get you a drink.

Just give me the cash — I'll get one later.

Excuse me: I don't normally talk to
strange women in the street, but
I'm on my way to confession
and I'm a bit short of material.

Try the draper's shop.

Let's eat out. How about Japanese?

I'm a bit short-sighted, so don't have the raw fish, or I won't know which end of you is which.

I'm fat, I'm ugly, I'm hairy, I'm smelly, and I fart like a wind tunnel. But I'm bloody rich.

I don't want you thinking I'm just after your money, darling. What's your name?

Hi. I'm on a computer date, actually, but the computer hasn't shown up. Do you want to join me instead?

No, I never date men with tiny peripherals.

Have you got any Irish in you?

No.

Would you like some?

Yes please. Mine's a Guinness.

Would you like another drink?

*Do you really think our relationship
will last that long?*

What's your favourite film?

Kodak.

What's your favourite flower?

Self-raising.

Do you believe in sex before marriage?

*In general, yes, but with you I'd make
an exception.*

Do you fancy coming for
a walk in the woods?

What for — to meet your family?

I want people to like me for what I am.

Is that why you drive a Porsche?

What's your favourite French dish?

Gerard Depardieu.

Have you had a wonderful evening?

Sure, but it wasn't this one.

If the world was an apple, you'd be the juicy pip, and I'd like to suck it.

The world isn't an apple. It's a planet, and planets don't have pips.

What's the best way to get into your affections?

Via the North Pole.

Are you a miner?

No.

Oh, so that's not a
pickaxe in your pocket?

What's your favourite record?

Sebastion Coe's 1500 metres.

I'm a photographer for a model agency:
I've been looking for a face like yours.

I'm a plastic surgeon.
I've been looking for a face like yours.

I've circumnavigated the
world single-handed.

What were you doing
with your other hand, then?

Cheer up darling,
it may never happen.

It just has.

Can you see me in your future?

No. You're already in my past.

With you I've finally found what I've been looking for in life.

With you I've finally lost it.

Kiss me and I'll tell you a secret.

I know your secret - I work at the clinic.

How do you keep
an idiot in suspense?

Don't know.

Nor me. Been waiting
for someone to tell me, actually.

Hello.

Goodbye.

BY THE SAME AUTHOR:

The Little Book of Flirting

Learn essential tips such as how to make your first impression count, when physical contact works (and when it doesn't), what to say and, more importantly, when to leave them guessing.

How to Chat-up Babes

Full of tips to boost your confidence with the opposite sex, no single bloke should enter a bar without this package tucked in his trousers.

The Little Book of Essential English Swear Words

Thicker, wider, longer lasting - yes, you too can have a vocabulary that impresses your friends, family and prospective employers.

www.summersdale.com